A. H. Moncur Sime

The Literary Life of Edinburgh

A. H. Moncur Sime

The Literary Life of Edinburgh

ISBN/EAN: 9783337415891

Printed in Europe, USA, Canada, Australia, Japan

Cover: Foto ©Thomas Meinert / pixelio.de

More available books at **www.hansebooks.com**

THE LITERARY LIFE
OF EDINBURGH.

By A. H. Moncur Sime.

LONDON: JAMES CLARKE & CO.
13 & 14, Fleet Street. 1898.

The Literary Life of Edinburgh.

THE literary history of Edinburgh, in any special sense, began about 1500. Before that time there was in manuscript only a good deal of scattered literary activity in Scotland generally, in which Edinburgh had shared, but in the reigns of James IV. and James V., dating from 1488 to 1542, Edinburgh became the central seat of literature in Scotland. The leaders in literature, the "Makars," as they were called, at this period were William Dunbar, Gavin Douglas, and Sir David Lyndsay.

1

The patent for establishing a printing - press in Scotland was granted in 1507 by the king, James IV., to one, Walter Chepman, a merchant, and another, Andrew Myllar, a working printer, both burgesses of Edinburgh. The "Golden Targe" and other poems, by Dunbar, were, so far as we can say, the first productions *Dunbar.* of the press. Dunbar was born in East Lothian not later than 1460. In 1475 he was at the University of St. Andrews, the oldest of the four Scotch Universities, evidently educating for the Church. For a time he seems to have worn the habit of the Franciscans, but he at length threw it off with disgust, since it had become to so many men a cloak of hypocrisy.

Good family connections, a liberal education, and rare natural ability, led to the employment of Dunbar as a servant of the King. During James's life, his home was almost constantly in Edinburgh. The King liked the poet's wit, saw him readily, and was familar with him. Dunbar's finest efforts are his "The Thrissel and the Rose," a poem celebrating the marriage of Margaret Tudor, daughter of Henry VII., to the Scottish King, and the "Golden Targe," which we have already mentioned. Both these works represent him very clearly as a student of Chaucer, and of the literature of the Middle Ages

Contemporary with Dunbar at the Court of James IV., but per- *Gavin Douglas.*

haps some fourteen years younger, was the poet Gavin Douglas, who lived to become a bishop. In 1501 or 1502 he was made Provost or Dean of the Collegiate Church of St. Giles in Edinburgh, a well-paid and important benefice, that brought him into close contact with the life of the Court. He had written the first of his poems, "The Palace of Honour," in 1501, and had dedicated it to the King. By far the most important literary work that came from Douglas's hands was his translation of Virgil's "Aeneid," which has led the way very worthily in the long line of Virgilian translation. It has freshness, vigour and native genius, and is altogether the production of a true poet. The description of a June evening in the " Vision of Maphaeus Vegius " —with its woods and streams, its cattle and meadows. its flowers and bees, the red sky with sun wholly on fire — lives in the memory of every poetic reader like some long happy summer day that has been really lived and felt.

Before the voice of Dunbar was quite silent Lyndsay had taken up the strain, and he struck notes of the deeper poetry of life. He was born about 1490. He also was in prominent service at the Scottish Court, though it does not appear that he belonged to the highest rank of the gentry. Lyndsay's sympathies were all with the people, and his writings

Sir David Lyndsay.

indicate pretty conclusively that
while taking part in the life of
the Court he never hesitated to
rebuke its vices and corruption.
He was a personal favourite with
King James V., but he did not
scruple to protest against his im-
morality and the flattery of his
false friends. He survived far
into the Reformation struggle,
and by his vigorous writings
against the tyranny of the Church
proved himself a notable ally of
Knox and other reformers. From
this time the temper of the
thought in Scotland generally, and
in Edinburgh as its centre, completely changed. The literary
history of Edinburgh at this
time is not without lustre, but
its literary life became wholly

merged in its political and religious life.

John Knox and George Buch- *John Knox and George Buchanan.* anan returned from their exile and wanderings on the Continent, and gathered round them the thoughtful and cultured of Edinburgh, but the thought was not that which buds and blossoms into poesy and writes itself into literature, but that which concentrates itself into character and expends itself in action. From 1580 to the beginning of the seventeenth century the literary history of Scotland is almost a blank page.

That period which in England was the golden age of literature, the Elizabethan age of peace and plenty, when " England became a nest of singing birds," saw Scot-

land grave and silent, steeped
heart and soul in the vexed and
momentous questions of religion
and of Church government, Pres-
byterianism *versus* Episcopacy,
and all the issues which to Scottish minds were of such serious
import, and to Scottish life of all-
engrossing interest.

The removal of the Court from
Edinburgh to London in 1603
still further deepened the gravity
of life in the capital north of the
Tweed, robbing it of the pageantry
which surrounds a Court, and
of the Court atmosphere which,
although it may not produce great
men or poets, always breeds
gallants and rhymsters.

It was in May, 1559, that Knox
finally landed at Leith, and became

the covenanted leader of the Re-
forming Party. The religious in-
stitutions raised to piety and learning were as guiltless of letters
as of godliness, and had become
nurseries of evil lives and indolence.
Society had become utterly care-
less of the ordinary rules of a
high morality, and Knox saw
clearly enough the danger of
leaving anything, either of the
government or worship of the
Church, which encouraged or
sheltered radical misconceptions
as to the meaning and end of
true religion. From 1559 till
his death in 1572 Knox laboured
unceasingly, and successfully, too,
we think, for the overthrow of
all injustice and wickedness in
the government of his native land.

The daily press was not then born, but he, by his sermons and addresses, did what is now done by editors in their columns, and by statesmen in their political campaigns. He sleeps within call of St. Giles's Church, that so often echoed to his words of strong sense and liberty. No monument but two letters and a date mark the resting-place of the man who, as Robert Louis Stevenson puts it, "made Scotland over again in his own image, the indefatigable and undissuadable John Knox." He wrote a great deal, mostly of a polemical character, and his style is terse, clear, and easy.

1589—
1700.

We have indicated the woeful change that had taken place in

the literary life of Scotland from 1580 onwards, and we can almost dispose in a sentence of the few individuals in this second period who are at all worthy of mention. Of these the most notable by far is William Drummond, of Haw- *William Drummond.* thornden, whose sonnets are admitted, on the highest literary authority, to be the best in the English language between the time of Shakespeare and that of Milton. Though not resident in Edinburgh, he was intimately associated with it, and he bequeathed his collection of books to the University of that city. He was a singer, sweet and pure. Could anything be prettier than that address to the lady who had been stung by a bee ?—

O, do not kill that bee
That thus hath wounded thee.
  Sweet, it was no despite
But hue did him deceive:
For, when thy lips did close,
He deemèd them a rose:
What wouldst thou further crave?
He, wanting wit, and blinded with delight,
Would fain have kissed, but, mad with
  joy, did bite.

Samuel Ruther-ford.

The only other names we would mention as belonging to this period are Samuel Rutherford, whose delightful letters have commanded a widespread renown on account of their deep spirituality and the beautiful and quaint diction in which they are couched,

Bishop Leighton.

and the good Bishop Leighton, of Dunblane, whose works, forty or fifty years ago, were widely known and highly prized.

1700—1786.

The literary revival in Scotland

came at the beginning of the eighteenth century, and it began with Allan Ramsay, a quaint, *Allan* shrewd little periwig maker of *Ramsay.* Edinburgh. A delightful, re- markable personage he would have been at any time, but coming, as he did, between two eras of Scottish literature, and forming the connecting link, he has had an interest and importance that his work alone might scarcely have won for him.

He was well fitted for the mission, uniting, as he did, a hearty patriotic admiration for the old native literature of Scot- land and a keen desire to see his country take her place again in the literature of the world.

He was the first, too, to make

it felt that the union of England
had not been a merely political one,
but that Scotland had a share too,
and by no means an unimportant
share, in the glorious literature
that England had been producing.
He himself was perfectly conscious,
in his own quaint way, of his
position and importance, and,
with a meagre interest in what
his English contemporaries were
doing, he was determined that
Scotland should show, too, what
she could do.

It was in 1712 that Edinburgh
recognised that in this little man,
who loved his ease and enjoyed an
evening's social intercourse and a
good laugh, she had a poet of her
own, and a worthy successor to
Sir David Lyndsay.

About that time a number of little pieces of verse came out in succession, in the form of humbly-printed leaflets, " by permission of the Easy Club," a small club of about a dozen persons of professed literary taste, of which club Ram-say was a member, and for which he had written these verses.

Between 1712 and 1718 he published several satires and moralisings, in rather crude English, under the influence of the Satirical School in London, also much better work in the colloquial Scotch of his own day, and a new edition, with several additional cantos of his poem, " Christ's Kirk on the Green."

By this time he had begun to combine bookselling with wig-

selling, removing with his family
to a house in High Street. Here
he spent eight prosperous and
happy years, enjoying his growing
reputation, which attracted to his
shop all the well-to-do and literary
residents in Edinburgh, and not
less his growing fortune, the fruit
of his double business and his
poetical work. He himself fully
appreciated the humour of his sit-
uation, as is evidenced in these
lines :—

I theek the out and line the inside
Of many a douce and witty pash [head]
And baith ways gather in the cash.

Nor did the humble citizens of
Edinburgh ignore the presence of
the poet in their midst. Busy and
economical housewives sent out
their children to bring them

Ramsay's latest piece, whatever it might be, which they eagerly read and enjoyed, and talked over with their neighbours. But Ramsay's fame was not merely local; it had penetrated to England, and in London his name was well known. In 1720, when he sent out subscription papers for a collected edition of his works, his appeal was immediately responded to. Dukes, earls, marquises, judges, lawyers, were among the subscribers, and some very widely known names were in the list, among others Alexander Pope, Sir Richard Steele, and Richard Savage.

In 1724 he still further enhanced his reputation by the "Tea Table Miscellany" and the

" Evergreen," a collection of Scots poems, written by the ingenious before 1600. In the following year he reached the zenith of his fame in his well-known and much-loved "Gentle Shepherd," a Scots pastoral comedy. It was received on all hands with enthusiastic admiration.

At this time, too, he embarked on a successful commercial enterprise by the establishment of a circulating library in Edinburgh. In 1728 and 1730 respectively, he published a second volume of poems and a collection of thirty fables; and thereafter he was content to rest on his well-won laurels.

For twenty-eight years he enjoyed the distinction of being a living literary celebrity, and his shop was one of the chief resorts and meeting-places of men of literary tastes, and was instantly sought out by distinguished visitors.

In 1736 Ramsay made a brave effort, and devoted much of his savings to establish a regular theatre in the Scottish capital. The enactment of a foolish statute almost immediately thereafter by George II. that there should be no performance of stage plays out of London and Westminster, save when the king chanced to be residing in another town, necessitated its being closed. Ramsay must have lost heavily, but he evidently soon tided over his loss, for in 1743 we find that he built a fine house for himself on the north

side of the Castle Hill, a curious
octagonal villa nicknamed by the
wags of the day " the Goose Pie "
and " the Bird's Cage," because of
a certain resemblance to these in
its shape. His entrance into it was
darkened for him by the death of
his wife, but for fourteen years he
lived in it with his two daughters,
charming and vivacious as ever,
full of enthusiasm and kindliness,
and greatly loved by all who came
in contact with him.

It is worthy of notice that the
morning star of that reformation
which has resulted in the universal
cheapening of literary publica-
tions was an Edinburgh bookseller of these times, one Alexander
Donaldson, who reprinted in Edinburgh, and sold in London,

English books, of which the
author's fourteen years' copyright
had expired.

Throughout the revival period so
brilliantly inaugurated by Ramsay
the hidden fires of literature that
had been stifled under the load of
the last century blazed forth in
many ways. Amid the many *David Hume.*
lights in the northern capital during our third period, there was no
brighter than David Hume, by far
the greatest philosophical writer
who had appeared since Berkeley.
He was the leader of the Utili-
tarians, and one of the greatest
critics of thought. Hume not
only made excursions into literature as an essayist, an historian,
and philosopher, but in all three
he is durably eminent.

He was a native of Edinburgh, and from childhood displayed a very strong inclination to books. When about eight-and-twenty he published his first work in two volumes, " A Treatise on Human Nature." It was far from being successful ; but a third volume, published in the following year, created considerable attention and discussion. Then some dozen years after appeared his " Political Discourses," which has really pointed the way for all future students of political economy.

By this time he would be about forty years of age. Through strict economy he had arrived at a sort of competence. He became librarian of the Advocate's Library, a post which was valued more for the opportunity it afforded for study than anything else, as the salary attached was paltry.

From 1751 till his death in 1776 Hume lived the greater part of his time in Edinburgh—part of the time in Riddel's Close, Lawn Market, now partly occupied by a band of æsthetic colonists, who are hoping in this way to influence the artistic sense lying dormant in the minds of the other occupants, people of a doubtful enough order, skulking gaol-birds, dirty, ragged, pilfering children, " big-mouthed, robust women, in a sort of uniform of striped flannel petticoat and short shawl."

It was from this quarter that he wrote in 1753 to a friend, describing his new home.

" I shall exult and triumph to you a
little that I have now at last, being
turned of forty—to my own honour, to
that of learning, and to that of the
present age—arrived at the dignity of
being a householder. About seven months
ago I got a house of my own, and com-
pleted a regular family, consisting of a
head, namely, myself, and two inferior
members, a maid and a cat. My sister
has since joined me, and keeps me
company. With frugality I can reach, I
find, cleanliness, warmth, light, plenty,
and content. What would you have
more? Independence? I have it in a
supreme degree. Honour? That is not
altogether wanting. Grace? That will
come in time. A wife? That is none
of the indispensable requisites of life.
Books? That is one of them, and I
have more than I can use. In short, I
cannot find any pleasure of conse-
quence which I am not possessed of in
a greater or less degree; and without
any effort of philosophy I may be easy
and satisfied. As there is no happiness
without occupation, I have begun a
work which will occupy me several

years, and which yields me much satis-
faction."

The work to which he here
refers was his famous " History of
Great Britain," the first volume of
which appeared in 1754.

Hume was miserably disap-
pointed at the reception his his-
tories met with.

There was a good deal about
Hume that repelled his fellow-
countrymen and townsmen. Still,
Edinburgh was very proud of her
gifted son, and there gathered
round him all the best society
of Edinburgh. That house of his
in James's Court—one of the
many-storeyed, sky-seeking build-
ing of the old city—was famous
indeed. Boswell and Blair lived
in the same tenement; Adam

Smith had his chamber in Hume's
flat; Benjamin Franklin was his
guest there for several weeks together.

Hume's agreeable and sociable
disposition, which grew more
striking with his years, gained for
him many friends, women as well
as men, and these he never failed
to please by his courtesy and
gentle raillery, which only amused
and delighted without ever wound-
ing even those against whom it
was directed.

We know how consistently and
doggedly atheistic he was, but he
never failed in courtesy and for-
bearance towards those who, even
in an obtrusive way, sought to
force views of an opposing character upon him.

A story from Hill Burton's
" Life of Hume " may fittingly
conclude our sketch of this remarkable man. In his last illness
a woman called upon him with
information that she had been
entrusted with a message to him
from on high. " This is a very
important matter, madam," said
the dying philosopher, " we must
take it with deliberation—perhaps
you had better get a little temporal
refreshment before you begin."
" Lassie," addressing his servant,
" bring this good lady a glass of
wine."

While the " good woman " was
preparing for the attack he good-
humouredly entered into conversation with her; and, discovering
that her husband was a chandler,

he announced that he was much
in want of some temporal lights at
that time, and entrusted her with
a large order. This unexpected
stroke of business completely di-
verted her thoughts, and, for-
getting all about her special
mission, she trotted contentedly
home to tell her husband the good
news.

In the latter part of the eighteenth century there was congre-
gated in Edinburgh a cluster of
brilliant men who made Edinburgh,
for the first time, the literary rival
of London. We can only give a
passing notice to a few of these.
A notable poet in the capital at
John   this period was John Home, the
Home.   author of " Douglas." Henry
Mackenzie, the biographer of

Home, known always as "the man of feeling," because he had published a novel with that title and had the title transferred to himself, took no small share in supporting the literary reputation of his country; and we should not forget that a review of the first edition of Burns's Poems, contributed by Mackenzie to "The Lounger," practically decided the fate and fame of the poet. Burns was on the point of emigrating when this article brought him into public notice, and secured him the help that encouraged his later efforts.

Adam Smith was resident in *Adam Smith.* Edinburgh for some twelve years, but his great book, a book which has, perhaps, done quite as much

for the good of humanity as any
other ever produced in Scotland,
was the work of ten quiet, studious
years previous to his coming to
Edinburgh. Smith was one of the
simplest and most retiring of men,
and some one has remarked that
it was strange how one who had
written so well on the principles
of exchange and barter was obliged
to get a friend to buy his horse
corn for him. The author of the
" Wealth of Nations " never
married. His household affairs
were managed by a Miss Jeanie
Douglas, a cousin of his own, of
whom he appears to have stood in
considerable awe. It is even said
that the amiable philosopher,
being fond of a bit of sugar, and
remonstrated with by her for tak-

ing it, would watch, and saunter backwards and forwards along the parlour floor till Miss Jeanie's back was turned in order to help himself to his favourite morsel.

Dugald Stewart, the famous *Dugald* professor of moral philosophy in *Stewart.* the University of Edinburgh, was another important figure in the literary life of this period. Lord Cockburn, who was one of his pupils, speaks of his ethical teaching as of great value, and says that whoever, either in the business of life or in the prosecution of philosophy, has occasion to recur to principles, always finds that either for study or practice Stewart's doctrines are his surest guides.

Stewart was one of the learned

men in Europe who refused to
give any countenance to the idea
that was then coming into view,
that language in its essential
principles was one. To say that
the classic tongues of Athens and
Rome had any kinship with "the
jargon of savages" was prepos-
terous. Stewart said there was no
such language as Sanskrit at all,
and he wrote his now incredible
essay to show how "those arch-
forgers and liars—the Brahmans,"
had tried to patch together a vast
imposition of language, after the
style of the Greek and Latin,
wherewith to deceive credulous
people.

His position seems to thoughtful men to-day incredible, and
would be amusing did it not warn

us of the lamentable errors into which even intelligent and learned men may fall through the blind leadership of prejudice and a too absolute devotion to a worn-out creed.

Robert Fergusson, the poet, *Robert Fergusson.* whose memory awakened in the breast of Burns an almost excessive passion of admiration and regret; Lord Monboddo, a judge of the Supreme Court and a man of great learning; James Boswell, the biographer of Johnson; and many more of scarcely less note, combined to make this third period in Scottish literary history full of activity and full of glory.

Hardly one of these men had adopted literature as a profession. When a Scotchman, then as now,

was led to adopt the literary profession out and out, he almost as
a matter of course migrated to
London, which was the centre of
the publishing world, and where
there was a literary market.

Perhaps it was this feature,
this absence of professionalism in
literature, which gave to the
literary society of Edinburgh its
special and peculiar tone and
characteristic. "Free and cordial
communications, the natural play
of good humour prevailed among
that circle of men," said Henry
Mackenzie.

These were the days which are
known, politically, as the time of
the Dundas despotism, the period
when Henry Dundas was the
actual dictator of Scotland and

the people had no voice in, and took no heed of, political matters. Dundasism was the political creed, and those who were wise in their generation simply professed it and were at peace.

Edinburgh was sociable in those days—more sociable than any place can well be nowadays, since the struggle for display has crept into society everywhere. " When shall I see Scotland again?" exclaimed Sydney Smith in one of his letters. "Never shall I forget the happy days passed there. My good fortune will be very great if I should ever again fall into the society of so many liberal, correct, and instructed men, and to live with them on such terms of friendship as I have done at Edinburgh."

Perhaps the most striking feature of Edinburgh society at that time was its intellectualism. Much strong and sound thought circulated at these free, delightful supper parties, contributed equally by men and women. Smith complained that the conversation ran too much to disputation and dialectic, insisting that many of the young ladies in Edinburgh did even their love-making in a metaphysical way. " I overheard," he says, " a young lady of my acquaintance, at a dance in Edinburgh, exclaim, in a sudden pause of the music, ' What you say, my lord, is very true of love in the aibstract, but '—here the fiddlers began fiddling furiously, and the rest was lost."

This fault of which Sydney complained probably owed something
to his wit, as well as to the little
peculiarities of the young ladies of
Edinburgh. That there was, however, a great deal of sententious-
ness and pompous parade of intellectualism, we have good proof in
a curious custom which prevailed
at this time. At dinner or supper
parties each guest, lady or gentleman, was expected, was indeed
required, to furnish what was
called a " sentiment "—that was,
a moral reflection of one kind or
another. Naturally enough, this
was a disquieting demand for the
timid and unready ; and in spite
of there being a large number of
stock " sentiments " available,
such as "May the distractions of

the evening bear the reflection of
the morning," the inexorable
demand for a "sentiment" was
often a source of much confusion
and distress. It is told of one of
the guests at such a gathering,
that his turn came, and found him
without any reflection, and, after
much writhing and agonising
under the collective eye of the
assembly, the unfortunate man
managed to stammer forth, "The
reflection of the moon in the calm
bosom of the lake."

It is not very probable that
such a custom would have origi-
nated in any country but Scotland,
and it is sure enough that it would
not have long survived anywhere
else.

"There has always been in

Edinburgh," says Professor Mas-
son, "a free under-current of
speculative opinion, a tough, tra-
ditional scepticism, a latitude of
jest at things clerical and presby-
terian. Towards the end of the
eighteenth century no city in
Britain sheltered such a quantity
of cosy infidelity." We question
the statement very much. Be that
as it may, however, there was cer-
tainly at that time much vigour
and independence of thought and
speech.

The debating societies, of which
the "Speculative," in connection
with the University, founded in
1764, was the chief, had bred
among the members habits of
independent thinking and free and
fearless debate. This critical

spirit, which had not yet found or
made organs for itself, permeated
the community.

Nor was this originality of
thought confined to young men.
At the close of the century, there
lived in the Old Town, mostly in
the Canongate, a race of old
ladies—a delightful set, strong-
headed, warm-hearted, high-
spirited, merry even in solitude,
resolute, indifferent to the modes
of the modern world, adhering to
their own ways, so as to stand out
like primitive rocks above modern
society. They belonged to good
old Scottish families, and were
intensely Scottish in their language
and habits. They were an important element in the life of the
city, and exercised a salutary and

delightful influence, being as caustic and unsparing in their speech as they were kindly in their thought and action.

Many are the anecdotes that are told concerning them. One of the most remarkable, Sophia Johnston, of the Hilton family, evidently inherited her originality from her father, for he, in order to see how she would turn out if left to herself, gave her no education whatever.

Sophia Johnston.

Sophia, thus cut off from ordinary sources of occupation, made herself a good carpenter and blacksmith, even shoeing horses occasionally till after middle life. When she became a woman she taught herself to read and write, and developed very good powers of intellect, so that her opinions, bluntly and forcibly expressed as they were, were deferentially accepted by men of high intellectual standing. Her dress was as peculiar as her character. When out of doors she wore a man's hat, and even when within a garment like a man's great coat, buttoned from the chin to the ground, thick worsted stockings, and strong shoes with brass clasps. And in this attire she sat in any drawing-room and at any table, amidst all the fashion and aristocracy of the land, and was welcomed and respected.

It is told of another of these old ladies, that once, when an audacious and rash young clergyman ventured to disagree with her

on some point of theology, she
drew herself up stiffly, and said,
with scathing emphasis, "Ye
speak, sir, as if the Bible had just
newly come out." One more
incident ere we bid these charming old ladies farewell. It is told
of the mother of Sir David
Dundas. One day her grand-
daughter was reading a newspaper
to her, and came to a paragraph
in which a lady's reputation suf-
fered rather severely through the
Prince Regent, by remarks passed
by himself. The old dame of
eighty sprang to her feet,
brandishing her silver-topped cane
furiously, and exclaimed "The
villain, does he kiss, and syne
tell."

An amusing story is told of

another of these old ladies in the
Canongate and a dream she had
of heaven. One morning she said
to a friend, "Eh, what a dismal
dream I had last nicht—it was
maist gruesome. I dreamt I was
in heaven, o' a' place on earth;
and the whole place was crowded
wi' stark naked weans. And ye
ken I never could abide bairns.
Eh, but it was a dismal dream."

1786—
1865.
In 1786 we get an interesting
little glimpse of the two men who
were to be the twin-lights, one
creative, the other critical, of the
giant epoch of literature in Edinburgh. It was in the winter of
that year that Burns, the famous
Kilmarnock edition of whose
poems had been published in

July, made his memorable visit to Edinburgh. In the house of Dr. Adam Ferguson, the historian of Rome, Burns happened to inquire the name of the author of some lines on a print which he had been inspecting. Nobody knew except one pale, lame boy, who, too modest to speak the name himself, whispered it to a friend near, who repeated it to Burns. The boy was Walter Scott. *Sir Walter Scott.*

About the same time, during this visit of Burns to the capital, another boy stood in the High Street, and stared at the striking figure of the poet. This was the boy who afterwards criticised and censured him so pitilessly—Francis Jeffrey.

Many of the biographers of Burns seem to imply, many of them indeed say it outright, that this visit of Burns to Edinburgh had a bad effect upon him, and made him discontented with his humbler state at home. We cannot for a moment think so. Burns was far too manly, and had too much insight, to be greatly affected by the enthusiasm of the passing hour. He himself best settles this matter, once for all, in a letter to a friend at Kilmarnock, in which he says:

" Novelty may attract the attention of mankind awhile—to it I owe my present fame—but I see the time not far distant when the popular tide, which has borne me to a height of which I am, perhaps, unworthy, shall recede and leave me a barren waste of sand to descend at my

leisure to my former station. I had
been at a good deal of pains to form
a just, impartial estimate of my intellectual powers before I came here; I
have not added, since I came to Edinburgh, anything to the account, and I
trust I shall take every atom of it back
to my shades, the coverts of my un-
noticed, early years."

In the year 1802 party feeling
ran very high in Scotland; and in
Edinburgh there was actual house-
to-house battle between the firmly-
rooted old Scottish Toryism, which
had received so overpowering a
blow in the downfall and expul-
sion from power of Dundas, and
the new Scottish Whiggism, which
claimed most of the rising younger
men in Edinburgh, with the notable exception of Scott.

The required party standard
was raised by the young Whigs.

Sydney Smith states its origin in his own characteristic way.

"Towards the end of my residence in Edinburgh, Brougham, Jeffrey, and myself happened to meet in the eighth or ninth storey or flat in Buccleuch-place, the then elevated residence of Mr. Jeffrey. I proposed that we should set up a review. This was acceded to with acclamation. The motto I proposed for the review was—"We cultivate literature on a little oatmeal."

But this was too near the truth to be admitted.

The time was ripe for a new publication, for there was an utter absence of enlightened public opinion. Consequently, the 10th of October, 1802, saw the first appearance of the "Edinburgh Review," of which, after the first few numbers, Jeffrey, who had been one of the most ener-

getic of its promoters, assumed
control.

Archibald Constable was the
publisher. He seemed to his
amazed fellow-citizens to have
passed almost at one step from
being a boy in Hill, the bookseller's shop, to an enterprising
publisher. Constable saw his
opportunity, and took immediate
advantage of it. He came for-
ward with such liberal and un-
heard of terms for a review, an
article, a poem, that he tempted
out all the talent that lurked in
Edinburgh, and very soon made
the capital a literary mart, famous
among strangers and the pride
and glory of its own citizens.
Edinburgh, from 1802 to 1832,
is often called the Edinburgh of

4

Walter Scott. His authorship
began in a peculiar and accidental
way enough. He made a translation from the German of Bür-
ger's "Lenore," and this translation he had made into a little
book, daintily printed and bound.
From this he stepped into the
"Border Minstrelsy," gaily scour-
ing the country in search of old
ballads.

His first original poem, "The
Lay of the Last Minstrel," was
written at the suggestion of one
of the ladies of the house of
Buccleuch, who told him the story
of the Elfin page, and begged
him to make a ballad of it.

Thus casually, and lightly, and
naturally did Scott step into literature. His original poem, pub-

lished in 1805, was an immediate
and complete success, and dis-
closed to him at once his power
and his field. The start made,
he proceeded rapidly and with
ever-increasing success, so that
his poetical work threw a literary splendour over the city.

Opinion was much divided as to
the superiority of Scott's poetry
or his talk. He is described as
being " most striking and delightful in society, where the halting
limb, the burr in the throat, the
heavy cheeks, the high Goldsmith
forehead, unkempt locks, and
general plainness of appearance,
Scottish accent, and stories and
sayings, all graced by gaiety,
simplicity and kindness, made an
enjoyable combination."

If we are to form our estimate
of Scott's character from the lov-
ing delineation of John Gibson
Lockhart, we must conclude that
among the splendid works of the
great enchanter there was none
greater or nobler than himself.
Scott's career as a novelist began
as unexpectedly, and with as little
premeditation, as his poetical.

He conceived the idea, by a
passing impulse, of writing a
prose story on the events of the
Rebellion of 1745. He showed
the MSS. to a friend, who read
it, and strongly advised the
author not to attempt story writing.

Scott accordingly tossed the
MSS. into a drawer, and there it
lay neglected, till he discovered

it some years later, when he was
looking for fishing tackle. He
read it over again, and thought
it not so bad as his friend had
said. The result was that in
1814 "Waverley" appeared. It
was received with a burst of
enthusiasm and delight.

In 1826 Constable's house
stopped payment; and the fail-
ure of the firm of Ballantyne, in
which Scott was involved for a
very large sum, followed immediately after. Scott's friends in
the Parliament House offered to
unite and give him what assist-
ance they could to help to clear
off his awful debt. He was
deeply moved by the offer, in
which opponents as well as
friends united. But "No," he

said, "this right hand shall work it all off"; and the result of his literary efforts from January, 1826, to January, 1828, brought close on £40,000 to his creditors.

Francis Jeffrey.

Francis Jeffrey made a good second to Scott in the literary history of Edinburgh at that time; and with his sharp look and manner, with few anecdotes and no stories, delighting in the interchange of thought and speculation, formed a great contrast to him.

In 1815 Jeffrey was at the height of his fame. No unofficial house in Scotland has had a greater influence on literary and political opinion than his. He had his little faults and foibles, but withal he was a brilliant

thinker and powerful critic. He
had a thorough scorn of mystifica-
tion either in men or books.

Carlyle speaks in a very kindly
way of Jeffrey, though you feel
the little sneer in such a remark
as "Jeffrey had much the habit
of flirting about with women,
especially pretty women, all in a
weakish, most dramatic, and
wholly theoretic way (his age now
fifty gone)," &c.

That Jeffrey could enjoy himself in a thoroughly simple and
natural sort of way, is indicated in
the report we have of a dinner in
the Assembly Rooms, in George-
street, which was held in honour
of Burns. Jeffrey's attitude towards Burns had, at least, con-
siderably modified by this time, so

we are not surprised to find him at such a gathering. Hogg, the " Ettrick Shepherd," author of many beautiful lyrics, was there, and acted as one of the croupiers. Dr. Morris, a Welsh physician, who was on a visit to Edinburgh, and who describes the scene, tells us he sang a Scottish song, the author of which he did not know. Hogg listened with growing excitement, edging his way nearer the singer, till at the close he seized his hand and exclaimed " Od, sir, Od, Dr. Morris, I wrote that song when I was a herd on Yarrow, and little did I think ever to live to hear an English gentleman sing it."

And so the full, hearty, glorious swing of jollity went on, hearts growing warmer, and heads not wiser, till communion of spirit had melted into confusion of spirits. One president gave way to another, till Patrick Robertson, who was the third or fourth, " made speeches, which, unlike epic poems, had neither beginning, middle, nor end; sang songs in which music was not; proposed toasts in which meaning was not." And the end of it all is not quite clear.

There were never many women of literary propensity or ability in Edinburgh. Mrs. Brunton, Mrs. Johnstone, and Miss Ferrier had published novels. Mrs. Elizabeth Hamilton, authoress of " The Cottagers of Glenburnie," a charming book; Mrs. Grant, of

Laggan, authoress of " Letters from the Mountains " ; Lady Nairne, the writer of the " Laird o' Cockpen," and the still more popular " Land o' the Leal," shared the honours of this period, and, despite the smallness of their means, their literary conversational gatherings were highly popular.

In the beginning of 1817 the first number of the " Scotsman " newspaper appeared. When it started it was published only once a week, and took only literary advertisements. It soon attained a very large circulation, and exercised considerable influence.

The only monthly periodical at this time was the old *Scots Magazine.* Constable changed its title

and structure, and William Black-
wood, an active and enterprising
bookseller, caught the opening for
a new venture. It became *Black-
wood's Magazine*, and was soon a
powerful organ. The famous
" Noctes Ambrosianæ " of Wilson *John*
(Christopher North) long enlivened *Wilson.*
its pages. These were a series of
scenes supposed to have occurred
in a tavern in Register Street,
kept by one Ambrose. It is a
singular and delightful outpouring
of criticism and politics, descrip-
tions of feeling, character, and
scenery, in prose and verse,
maudlin eloquence and wild fun.

Wilson himself was one of the
most remarkable-looking men in
the city, and has been described
as looking " like a fine Sandwich

Islander who had been educated in the Highlands."

Carlyle's share in the literary life of Edinburgh was not a very large one. In 1820 he was discovered by Sir David Brewster, and was employed by him on the Edinburgh Encyclopædia, which Brewster had begun to edit in 1810. In 1820 George IV. paid a visit to Edinburgh, an event which is not of much importance to us, save as it illustrates the different characters of two of Edinburgh's greatest men. Scott was greatly excited over the event, and took a large share in the preparation and the decorations in honour of it, and played his part in the pageantry and enjoyed the bustle and the stir. Carlyle, with his fierce democratic feelings, fled for a week to Annandale, to be quite out of sight and hearing of all the foolishness and empty show.

An anecdote relating to this journey must not be forgotten. On his way to Annandale he put up for the night at a little country inn. The partitions were thin, and in the room next to him a woman suffering from toothache, or some other pain, groaned ceaselessly, so that she "murdered sleep" for poor Carlyle. He knocked on the partition as an intimation to her that she was disturbing his rest, but this had no effect. So at last he shouted— "For God's sake, woman, can you not cease that groaning? If anything can be done for you, though

it be to ride ten miles in the dark
for a doctor, say so, and it shall
be done. If not, endeavour to
compose yourself." The rebuke
was effectual, and the groaning
ceased. So like Carlyle; and the
last touch is very characteristic.

In 1827 he formed his memorable acquaintance with Jeffrey,
and thereafter, by contributions to
the *Edinburgh Review* and other
periodicals, his prospects became
much brighter. He also became
acquainted with Sir William
Hamilton, then Professor of
Logic, whom he had previously
admired from a distance, often, as
he tells us himself, watching the
light in Hamilton's window, and
thinking of the earnest philosopher at work within that lighted

room. One other frequent visitor at the Carlyles' house in Comely Bank was that most fascinating and most graceful of writers, De Quincey, whose sojourn in the northern city was chequered in the extreme.

De Quincey.

Carlyle, in his own grim way, thus speaks of this altogether remarkable man as he knew him in 1827:—

" He is one of the smallest men you ever in your life beheld, but with a most gentle and sensible face, only that the teeth are destroyed by opium, and the little bit of underlip projects like a shelf. He speaks with a slow, sad, and soft voice, in the politest manner I have almost ever witnessed, and with great gracefulness and sense. were it not that he seems decidedly given to prosing. Poor little fellow, it might soften a very hard heart to see him so courteous, yet so weak and poor, tottering home with his two children to a miserable lodging-house, and writing all day for that prince of donkeys, the proprietor of *The Saturday Post.*"

We must not forget, as belonging to the latter part of our fourth period, Hugh Miller, eminent in journalism, but far more widely known in connection with geological science; Dr. Thomas Chalmers, a gifted and voluminous writer, but a genius for organisation, and one of the greatest pulpit orators of modern times; and the brothers William and Robert Chambers, who, against tremendous odds, fought their way to the front rank of journalism, and have left a name, not less renowned for integrity and goodness, than for literary judgment and remarkable business talent.

As links between the fourth

Hugh Miller.

Thomas Chalmers.

William and Robert Chambers.

period and our own day, we can only name Dr. John Brown, who for many years was one of the most distinguished and best-loved literary men in Edinburgh, and whose inimitable sketch of " Rab and his Friends " is known where-ever the English language is spoken; John Stuart Blackie, the man of the plaid and stick, the poet, philosopher, and educational-ist; and another, whose name is worthy to stand among the many who have brought honour to their fatherland by their genius and their patriotism — a very king in the realm of letters—Robert Louis Stevenson.

And with Stevenson we reach the end of our survey, though not the end of our subject. The

John Brown.

John Stuart Blackie.

Robert Louis Steven-son.

5

literary life of Edinburgh is not ended, but the life of the present is a story for the future.

There are not wanting many who tell us that the literary glory of Edinburgh has died out, that kings of thought and princes of poesy tread her streets, and adorn her law courts, and thunder from her pulpits, and speak from her professional chairs, with voice that reaches far beyond her bounds, no more.

The past is past, and it produced great giants. We know them, know their height, their power, their achievement. But how unjust to measure our growing men against those whom death has stretched and time has measured.

We revere the mighty dead,

but our hope is in those whose last
word has not been spoken, and in
those whose first word has yet to
be written. In the historic and
sacred graveyards of old Edinburgh rest many of her great sons,
but in her streets, among the
living, who can tell that we do not
brush heedlessly by some Scott
whom happy fortune has not yet
led into his kingdom, some Carlyle
frowning out upon the world from
beneath his load of thought.

Edinburgh has every require-
ment for the centre of a Scottish
literature, with her grand historic
objects and grander associations,
with her stirring and varied
memories and her unquestioned
power; but she does not recognise
her possibility, neither does she

make provision for those who might make her glorious.

Are these not times that can produce great men as well as the time gone by? Or, is it that now and then great men come, and make their times great? History answers "Yes" to both. The mighty in literature are those who translate the feeling of their time and of their nation into thought and give it to the world.

They are the product of their time, but the shapers of it also, for they give it a new impetus, and a new direction.

Scotland is ripe for a revival of Scottish literature, a national literature that shall embody the spirit that animates Scotsmen, the

spirit that has made Scotland
what it is.

The genius of Scottish literature
is something far other and something far greater than a happy
trick of the vernacular ; something far wider than local sentiment and thought, whether these
be accurately produced or no.

True Scottish literature needs
the ancient capital for a foster-
mother to give it dignity, and to
call forth its best and richest
power, and Edinburgh is well
fitted for the task. But Edinburgh
must tempt them to her by her
provision for them; she must make
room for proud, philosophic
thought that knows its worth and
will not truckle nor scramble for
place; she must prepare a hearty

welcome for the shy muse of poesy that plays like a sunbeam around and above its common life and with sudden, striking ray pierces into the heart of it.

Then shall her old-time glory be regilded, and she shall make it clear that—

The present moves attended
By all of brave, and excellent, and fair
That made the past time splendid.

www.ingramcontent.com/pod-product-compliance
Lightning Source LLC
Chambersburg PA
CBHW022150090426
42742CB00010B/1459